"Ottsen has given us a wondrous gift. From his deep well of pastoral experience, he offers us Jesus' great invitation: 'Come to me, all of you that are weary and are carrying heavy burdens.' He explains in depth what this invitation means, how we can respond to it in our own lives, and what it looks like when we live it out in practice . . . *The Greatest Invitation* is practical, positive, and empowering!"

—EDWARD S. LITTLE
Author of *Joy in Disguise*

"*The Greatest Invitation* is like a seed: small, but packed with a plan. Clearly and simply written, it is a thoughtful yet practical four-step guide for those who would divest themselves of spiritual burdens. Can we rise above our circumstances and positively transform our lives? This little book lends us hope and provides a pathway to do just that."

—WENDY ISAAC BERGIN
Author of *The Threshold of Eden*

"Meditating upon the great invitation by Jesus, Ottsen has created a complete set of exercises to help the spiritual pilgrim breathe a new kind of air—one of rest, joy, and love. This will be a resource for spiritual directors and those searching for the peace of Jesus that passes all understanding."

—C. ANDREW DOYLE
Author of *Citizen: Faithful Discipleship in a Partisan World*

"*The Greatest Invitation* is skillfully written, spiritually inspired, and has simple skills and techniques to help take the yoke and burdens out of our lives. As a social worker and minister, I loved the individual stories and case scenarios. With so many fighting anxiety, depression, discouragement, stress, suicide, and many other social and spiritual issues, this book is especially timely."

—RANDY WELLS
Executive Director, Faith Mission, Brenham, Texas

"Simple and powerful. David Ottsen not only exhorts us to embrace the great invitation but provides practical actions for our own journey to joy."

—**SANDRA DAVIS**
Author of *Pearls of Leadership Wisdom*

The Greatest Invitation

The Greatest Invitation

Your Handbook for Hope

David Ottsen

RESOURCE *Publications* · Eugene, Oregon

THE GREATEST INVITATION
Your Handbook for Hope

Resource Publications
An Imprint of Wipf and Stock Publishers
199 W. 8th Ave., Suite 3
Eugene, OR 97401

www.wipfandstock.com

PAPERBACK ISBN: 978-1-6667-3126-2
HARDCOVER ISBN: 978-1-6667-2358-8
EBOOK ISBN: 978-1-6667-2359-5

10/18/21

The Scripture quotations contained herein are from the *New Revised Standard Version Bible*, ©1989, Division of Christian Education of the National Council of Churches of Christ in the U.S.A. Used by permission. All rights reserved.

The poem by Spenser J. Somers at the end of Part Three is from his book, *Eating LIFE® Cereal with a Bigger Spoon Than Most*. It is used here with permission. The book, published by Life's Destinations Co., is copyright ©1997 by Karen S. Somers and John O. Somers

Polly's account in Part Two is used here by permission.

The stories recounted in this book are all true, taken from the life experiences of real people. In most accounts, names (and in some cases a few details) were changed to honor people's privacy. Where real names are used, permission from each was provided.

To my wife, Deborah, my beloved,
without whose encouragement and challenge, love and support,
this book could never have happened.

Contents

Acknowledgments

I want to thank all who helped me write and re-write this book; who gave me permission to use their stories; or who, in any way, encouraged, supported, or productively challenged me. I especially want to thank:

- Polly, who inspired me to begin, and for permitting me to use her story
- Don, Ann, and Linda, in providing inspiration and transformative experiences from their lives
- Clare, Doug, Jerry, and Wendy, for their suggestions, thoughts, and encouragement in working through early drafts
- Brent, for providing his expertise in Scripture
- Carrie, for her clarifications on grammar
- Sandra, for her support in so many ways
- Scott, for his professional advice, direction, and guidance
- Deborah, for her persistence in keeping me moving forward.

Most importantly, I acknowledge the grace of God in and for The Greatest Invitation.

There are times in life when our weariness and burdens are overwhelming. The weight becomes unbearable, bending our backs and crushing our spirits. If you are

- *utterly exhausted*
- *completely worn out*
- *despairing under the weight of your burdens, or*
- *immobilized, and find it impossible to move without adding to your burdens*

please turn immediately to Part Two.

How This Book Can Help

Do you wish there was a way to reduce your weariness? Do you long for release from the weight of your burdens? Do you dream of a time when you don't feel so worn out? Do you wonder if there can ever be a time when just thinking about your burdens doesn't add to them?

If you answered "yes" to any of these questions, The Great Invitation is for you.

You, and I, and all of us, do not need to live under the weight of our weariness and burdens. We are all offered The Great Invitation, which leads to a different, hope-filled way of life.

By accepting The Great Invitation, you can grow toward becoming the person you desire to be. You can develop relationships that are richer and deeper, and that create more space in yourself for peace and hope. You can develop the virtues that enable your humanity to shine.

This book is your guide to experiencing the release, relief, and hope of The Great Invitation.

This book is divided into three parts. Part One presents and examines the source and content of The Great Invitation. Part Two offers ways of responding positively to it. Part Three offers glimpses of what accepting The Great Invitation can mean for you.

One caveat before beginning: living into The Great Invitation does not dismiss our obligations or excuse us from our responsibilities. Instead, living into The Great Invitation unburdens us, and

The Greatest Invitation

transforms our way of living so that we can address our obligations and responsibilities in a new, hope-filled manner.

David Ottsen
October 2021

You Are Invited

THIS BOOK IS ABOUT The Great Invitation. It is both a general invitation, made to everyone, and a personal one, meant for each of us—and for you. Though it was made a couple of millennia ago, it is still fresh and powerful today:

> *Come to me,*
> *all you that are weary and are carrying heavy burdens,*
> *and I will give you rest.*
> *Take my yoke upon you, and learn from me;*
> *for I am gentle and humble in heart,*
> *and you will find rest for your souls.*
> *For my yoke is easy, and my burden is light.*
> —Jesus of Nazareth
> (Matthew 11:28–30)

There are only two things that matter in this Great Invitation:

- You are weary and carrying heavy burdens.
- Jesus invites you to give those burdens to him.

Whether you are Christian, Jewish, Muslim, the adherent of some other religion, agnostic, or a professed atheist, it does not matter. There is no expiration date or limited service area, so you may accept The Great Invitation at any time, wherever you are.

This Great Invitation is offered to *every* human being who is weary and carrying heavy burdens.

PART ONE

Receiving The Great Invitation

WHILE MOST INVITATIONS NEED no explanation, The Great Invitation requires one, for two reasons.

First, because it bears Jesus' name, it can raise suspicion, barriers, or opposition, especially among non-Christians.

Some people may only be aware of Jesus through what they have heard or seen in the press, on television, in movies, or on the internet—or through the words of religious writers who misunderstand The Great Invitation.

Others may have been hurt by some Christians who have misused or abused Jesus' name and teachings.

Others point to certain sayings of Jesus that call for some specific commitment to him, some belief about him, or some faith-based response to him.

Indeed, there *are* some other teachings of Jesus that call for such responses. But The Great Invitation includes no such requirement.

If any of the above descriptions resonates with you, I offer you my own invitation to keep reading. As you will see, Jesus' Great Invitation is meant for each and all of us—not just believers, followers, or Christians.

Second, the breadth and depth of The Great Invitation is so expansive, so all-encompassing, and so all-inclusive that it may seem unbelievable or unreal. I assure you that it is neither.

Its breadth and depth ensure that no human being who is weary and heavily burdened is omitted from The Great Invitation. Its breadth and depth also underscore the completeness of the hope it provides.

This invitation is not called The Great Invitation because I believe it is great. It is called The Great Invitation because it extends to the full breadth of humanity, and reaches into the depths of being in each one of us.

Understanding the Words and Phrases of The Great Invitation

Come to me

At first glance, this phrase might seem arrogant, even condescending. Yet we commonly say similar things to each other every day out of simple human compassion.

BETH ANN AND LAURA

Beth Ann, a single mom with young children, felt stressed out and overburdened. In a conversation with her good friend Laura, Beth Ann could not help but talk about her weariness and sense of being weighed down.

Laura quickly recognized Beth Ann's plight. She said, "It sounds to me like you need a break. So, one day in the next weekend or two—your choice—come on over. We have a pool; the children can go swimming or just play. You can join them, take a nap, read a book, whatever. No pressure; it's just a time to refresh and relax. You don't need to bring anything other than swimsuits. We have extra towels, so no need to go home and do more laundry. Just come on over."

D'ANDRE

D'Andre was driving home on a bitterly cold morning after a snowstorm. As the wind whipped the snow in spirals, he saw a woman trudging down the sidewalk, burdened with a large bag of groceries. He pulled over and offered her a ride. "Come on in out of the cold," he said. "I'll drive you where you're going."

At first the woman was suspicious of a stranger offering her a ride. But after some conversation, in which D'Andre made it clear that he wanted nothing from her and was truly just offering help, she accepted his invitation, and he took her home.

Like the phrases in these two stories—*Come on over* and *come on in out of the cold*—Jesus' words, *Come to me*, express his straightforward compassion for the well-being of others, including you.

All

The Great Invitation is given to everyone, to *all*. Jesus sets no limitations on who may come to him.

Black, white, red, yellow, and brown may come. Rich and poor and everyone in between may come. Young and old, healthy and ill (no exclusion for pre-existing conditions) may come. Those who can walk, and those who can't, may come. The intelligent and the mentally challenged may come. Those weighed down by their past, those who curse their present, and those who think they have no future may come.

Whether you are salaried, or work by the hour, or own your own business, or are unemployed, or are retired, you are invited. Whether you are married, partnered, or single, you are invited. If you are struggling with relationships, loneliness, gender identity, or anything else, you are invited. If you question your own or others' value, you are invited. If you have doubts about Christianity or religion in general, you are invited.

The Great Invitation isn't just extended to Jesus' followers. It is offered to everyone who is curious about Jesus; to those who see him only as a prophet or rabbi; and even to those who oppose him. So, whether you converse with Jesus regularly, feel unworthy to acknowledge him, or have never given him the time of day, you are invited.

When Jesus made The Great Invitation, he was speaking to a large crowd. Among them were not only his followers, but casual observers, curious onlookers, and people who doubted or opposed him. Yet he didn't add any qualifying or exclusionary words to his Invitation. Jesus didn't exclude *anyone*. He intended The Great Invitation for everyone, those present then and those in the future—including you.

AKIRA AND MASARU

Akira and Masaru had been close friends for many years. But over the past several months, Akira had been complaining to Masaru more and more. He complained about his health, his job, his parents, his wife, his apartment—sometimes even about his cat.

One day, as Akira began to recite his usual litany of complaints yet again, Masaru interrupted, "Akira, stop! I've been listening to you complain for months. When are you going to do something about your issues?"

Akira responded, "I've tried! But nothing has worked."

Masaru said, "Well, then, let me suggest that you pray to Jesus about your dilemmas."

Akira looked blankly at his friend. He sighed and said, "You know I don't believe. So why would I pray about it? And why would I pray to Jesus?"

"I know you don't believe," Masaru said. "You've told me that many times. But you aren't getting anywhere. It looks to me like things are getting worse. So, all I'm suggesting is that you pray to Jesus about your burdens. If nothing happens, then you haven't lost anything. And if something does, then won't you be better?"

Akira was silent for a while. Then he finally said, "I'll think about it."

Akira did more than think about it. Later that evening, when he was reeling under the weight of his burdens, he recalled Masaru's suggestion. *Well,* he thought, *what have I got to lose?* He did pray. It was a simple prayer in which he acknowledged his burdens and asked Jesus to help. That first prayer led to another, and then another.

Steadily, good things—even amazing things—began to happen in his life. His supervisor at work, who had been a relentless source of problems, suddenly left for a different job, and the person who became the new supervisor was someone Akira greatly respected. Soon after that, adjustments were made to his job that made it suit him much better.

A continuing disagreement with his landlord, which had been a source of great frustration for Akira, was suddenly and surprisingly resolved when the landlord offered him a larger apartment for the same rent.

Once he and his wife no longer felt like sardines in a can, they began to work together in positive ways to resolve some of their family issues.

Masaru knew things were changing for the better when Akira not only stopped repeating his litany of burdens, but actually began joking about his cat. He felt like he had his old friend back again.

JULIO

When Julio was young, he was a committed Christian and an active church member. But as more struggles and difficulties arose in his life, they eventually began to overwhelm him. Julio quit going to church and his once-active prayer life withered.

As the months passed, those struggles intensified. Julio responded by trying harder and harder to overcome them on his own, while drifting further and further away from his former congregation, as well as from Jesus. Eventually his normal Sunday morning routine involved staying at home—drinking coffee, having breakfast, and reading the news on his tablet.

The Greatest Invitation

One Sunday morning, as he was enjoying his coffee and catching up on the news, he heard an internal voice urging him to go to church. At first he tried to ignore it, but the voice kept returning.

So, he went to church that morning. Almost immediately, he felt at home once again. And in the middle of the service, he found himself thinking, *Jesus, please help me. I'm so tired—and so sick of all the troubles in my life.*

After the service, Julio pulled the pastor aside and said to her, "I have to tell you what happened this morning. As I was reading the news and drinking my coffee, Jesus kept pushing me to be here. Even after all this time, and with all the garbage going on in my life, I came. And I want you to know that I'm so glad I did. I can't begin to describe the peace I'm feeling. It's a peace I haven't known in a long, long time."

No matter what condition you're in, and no matter what your relationship with Jesus is—even if you dislike him—*nothing* changes Jesus' Great Invitation that *all* may come to him.

Who are weary and are carrying heavy burdens

The Great Invitation is offered to any and every human being who is weary or carrying heavy burdens. Isn't this everyone? Is there anyone who hasn't felt this way at some point?

Jesus doesn't describe or define what he meant by "weary and carrying heavy burdens." He doesn't set *any* parameters or limitations on what those need to be.

You determine whether you are weary and carrying burdens. If you are weary in any way, then The Great Invitation is meant for you. If you carry any kind of heavy burden, then The Great Invitation is extended to you.

Your burdens need not be numerous or extreme, though often they are. Sometimes a single burden can weigh us down and immobilize us.

Your weariness need not be only physical. Mental, emotional, and spiritual weariness are included in The Great Invitation.

Your weariness can be a response to *anything*. For example:

- ongoing struggles in a relationship
- the stress of needing to perform at work, in the classroom, or on the athletic field
- the daily commute to and from school or work
- the grind of making a living and/or feeding and raising a family
- a problem or conflict that seems unsolvable
- a person who regularly creates difficulty in your life
- a persistent health issue for you or someone in your family
- having little or no time for yourself
- negative external messages borne of racism, or sexism, or misogyny, or homophobia
- negative internal messages undermining your value
- the incessant, blaring chorus of conflicting voices in the media, in advertising, and almost everywhere else.

The Great Invitation also applies to every type and size of burden, such as:

- a past or present loss in your life that is yet to be healed
- an unresolved matter at work or in a relationship
- an unfulfilled dream or goal
- caring for someone who is dependent upon you
- never finding the answer to the question *What's my life all about?*
- the strains and struggles of living into your identity
- the hurt and pain you may have caused others
- the hurt and pain others may have caused you
- the hurt and pain you may have caused yourself
- the weight of guilt or regret.

It's important to mention one very common, and often very heavy, burden here: painful memories. No matter how much time may have passed since the original event, these memories can compound the weariness and burdens you bear. This is true even of memories you do not consciously remember.

Depending upon what those memories hold, you may need to seek specialized help—such as a counselor or therapist—for healing them.

Nevertheless, The Great Invitation also extends to the weariness and burdens caused by such memories.

JOHN, TOM, AND MARY ANN

For years, John suffered from painful back problems, which caused him to become more and more bent over. Eventually he was told that he needed back surgery, which he scheduled. While he understood the need for the surgery, he nevertheless felt worn out and overburdened.

John asked a few people to come to his house and pray for him on the night before the surgery. Among that group were Tom and Mary Ann, who were noted for their gift of healing.

After some time of praying together, the group stopped for a break. As they did, Tom thought, *Nothing is happening. It doesn't seem like we have any direction or focus.*

A few minutes later, Mary Ann heard an inner voice repeat, over and over, a single word: *airplane.*

As the group gathered to pray again, Mary Ann asked, "John, does the word 'airplane' mean anything to you?"

John immediately burst into huge, heaving sobs. Tears poured down both cheeks as if his face were a fountain. Everyone was stunned.

For the next few minutes, Tom and Mary Ann stood by John and rubbed John's shoulders, while he cried into his cupped hands.

After his crying finally subsided, and John was able to fully catch his breath, he explained: "In World War II, I was a bombardier. I was the one who pushed the button that released the bombs. Sometimes those bombs I released hit hospitals, schools, playgrounds, and hundreds of houses. Ever since then, I've felt enormous guilt and grief, every single day."

Tom said to John, "I—we—want to help you. But I need you to do something first. I need you to close your eyes and imagine that you're back on that plane, flying a bombing run. Can you do that, John?"

John cautiously nodded his head, squeaked out a "yes," and closed his eyes.

"Good" Tom said quietly. "Now, can you see Jesus anywhere on that plane?"

At first John sat motionless and said nothing. But then he moved a bit in his chair and replied, to his own amazement, "Yes."

"Where is he?"

"He's standing right behind me." Brushing back new tears, John added, "He's whispering something in my ear."

"What is he whispering?" Tom asked.

John was silent for a few moments. Then, in a halting manner, he said, "He's saying, 'I'm with you John. I'll take your hurt and pain.'"

Tom rubbed John's shoulders some more, letting the silence that followed seep into everyone. Then he said to John, "Thank you, John. Well done. You can open your eyes now."

Then, turning to the group, Tom said, "Now we have our focus in praying for John—letting Jesus take his hurt and pain."

The next day John went in for his surgery, and a radiologist took a final set of x-rays. After viewing the x-rays, the surgeon sat with John and told him, "I'm cancelling your surgery for today. We can't explain it, but your back is healing. We want to wait and see what happens. If this continues, you won't need surgery at all."

John's back did continue to heal, and he never needed the surgery. The weight had been lifted, the burden taken away.

. . . and I will give you rest . . .rest for your souls

The rest that Jesus speaks of goes far beyond relaxation or even refreshing sleep—though the rest he gives includes both.

The rest Jesus gives permeates our whole being. It brings restoration to our body, tranquility of mind, and serenity of spirit. This rest conveys refreshment and renewal.

In this rest we discover not simply the absence of anxiety and dread, but the active presence of peace: *the peace of God, which surpasses all understanding* (Philippians 4:7). This peace empowers us with hope.

JAZMIN

Jazmin took a job at a big tech company because she felt it offered so much promise. But over time, things started unraveling—and never stopped.

The problem was with Paul, her co-worker. At first, they worked well together as a team. But as the months passed, for reasons Jazmin never could determine, Paul became progressively more upset with her.

After a year, their relationship had devolved into a mutual lack of trust. Paul rebuffed all her attempts to make things better. His communications were terse, and they often contained unwarranted back-biting comments. Eventually Jazmin understood that things would only keep getting worse, and she left the company.

But even after Jazmin changed jobs, she found herself unsettled and burdened by her experience with Paul, and weary from its memory. She knew she needed to forgive him in order to heal—and there were many times she tried. But every time she recalled the job, or her interactions with Paul, she found herself wracked with hurt and pain all over again. She'd stop herself from thinking about it for a while, but it always sprang up again within a few days. The cycle kept repeating. She was going in circles and she knew it.

One Sunday morning, she arrived early for church and sat down by herself in the chapel. Her thoughts soon drifted back to that painful experience yet again.

But, on this morning, Jazmin remembered the words of The Great Invitation. Immediately, she took them to heart. She gave to Jesus every part of that work relationship, and every painful event that had occurred. She gave Jesus her weariness, her strivings to forgive, and the pain she felt in every memory. She whispered into the quiet, "I don't want to carry this anymore. Help me. Help me forgive."

As the words passed her lips, Jazmin immediately felt the tension in her body lessen. Over the next few minutes, with each breath she took, she felt peace and refreshment grow in her.

After a deep sleep that Sunday night, she awoke completely refreshed and renewed on Monday morning.

This is the rest Jesus promises us—promises you—when you accept The Great Invitation.

For my yoke is easy and my burden is light.

These phrases seem like contradictions. How can a yoke be easy? What burden is light? When have *yoke* and *easy,* or *burden* and *light,* ever been linked together? How and why is it that Jesus puts them together?

The Easy Yoke

The yoke that Jesus would have us wear is the joy of the presence of God. It is not a brutal yoke—unplaned, rough, heavy, and cumbersome. This yoke is smooth and contoured to fit our own spirit. It is personalized for each of us. It bears the graces of God's presence: love, joy, peace, patience, kindness, generosity, faithfulness, gentleness, and self-control (Galatians 5:22–23).

This yoke bestows upon us the power and strength of God. It transforms the way we live, so that in any situation, at any time, and in any place—no matter what is happening or how we feel—God's presence reminds us that we are neither alone nor powerless. God is with us. The fullness of this yoke is now revealed: we are carried *by* the yoke.

ELIZABETH

Elizabeth survived the tyrannical regimes of Idi Amin and Milton Obote in Uganda. Both men had ravaged the country. Schools and libraries were closed, and many were burned to the ground. Many citizens, including religious leaders, were rounded up and executed. Outside of the capital city of Kampala, where Elizabeth lived, there was little electricity, little running water, and almost no health care. Intimidation and fear were everyone's constant companions.

After these terrible regimes ended, conditions were slow to improve. The climate of fear and danger continued to shroud many citizens' daily lives.

Yet, despite these conditions, people who met Elizabeth found her filled with joy and the love of God. She emanated God's peace in the very way she lived. She regularly helped those in need around her, especially children. As she did, she radiated joy, love, and peace. Though she was entirely realistic about her situation and her country's condition, she lived a life of hope and goodness.

Day by day, and moment after moment, Elizabeth was carried by the yoke of God's presence. She explained it this way: "It would be easy to be overwhelmed by everything that isn't right in my country and in my life. But Jesus always makes it possible to experience joy. I'd rather wear that."

The Light Burden

The burden Jesus would give us is the burden of love. This burden is light because love conveys a lightness of spirit, instills in us energy for living, and creates strength of will.

This burden is light not only in the sense of weight. It also provides illumination. We become empowered to see our life more clearly—our relationships, our challenges, our fears, our delights, the path before us, and our own heart. This light draws us further into love itself, bringing the illumination of hope to every aspect of our life.

ALYSSA

Alyssa, a wife and mother of two young children, suffered from a quickly worsening form of ALS. Despite doctors' efforts, over the past several months her downward spiral continued. She had to move to a nursing home, where she could receive 24/7 care. Talk about being weary and carrying a heavy burden!

As the disease progressed, she created a short prayer that, even in her weakening state, she could think and say in a single breath. It became a prayer for the whole family—one they all recited, both together and individually. They called it "Mom's Prayer," and it conveyed God's all-embracing love for all of them.

Alyssa, her husband, and her two children prayed her prayer many times a day. God's love soon permeated not only their hearts, but Alyssa's room at the nursing home—and anywhere else in the facility where Alyssa and her family went. Visitors and medical staff could feel that love.

Eventually, Alyssa almost completely stopped speaking and could barely move. When it became clear that her death was drawing near, her family formed a circle around her bed.

Just before her last breath, with her husband and two children by her bedside, Alyssa suddenly whispered her final words: "It's so beautiful!"

The love of God did more than just lighten Alyssa's burden. It enabled her to see beyond her illness. In her final minutes, it enabled her to see beyond this Earthly life—and it gave her the strength to witness to her family the splendid sight before her. The love of God carried Alyssa to her beautiful end.

Responding to The Great Invitation

As you make your way through Part Two, please take note
of the boxes, like this one, at the end of each section.

How CAN WE ACCEPT the Great Invitation?

Some people find acceptance quickly—through a sudden insight or realization, or an opening of their hearts, or a gift of grace.

For most people, though, acceptance happens through a process. One event or act gives birth to something new, which in turn leads to something else new—and the process continues.

Part Two of this book describes a process of four steps in accepting The Great Invitation, as well as some common challenges in accepting it. This description is not meant to add to your weariness or burdens. I offer it so that you may understand each step well, and be better equipped to move through these steps into hope.

The steps are the same, no matter how deep your weariness is or how large your burdens are. Though these steps can often be completed in fairly short order—in some rare cases, even in a single profound insight—the time frame will vary from person to person, and from occasion to occasion.

I've presented the four steps in a specific order. Yet not everyone experiences a clear, step-by-step sequence. You may find yourself moving back and forth between steps—or living into more than one step at a time. The details of your process, the time frame, and the rhythm of change and acceptance, will be uniquely yours.

The four steps are guideposts. Use the steps in whatever way best helps you lay down your weariness and burdens and release them to Jesus. That is the point of The Great Invitation.

At first, these steps may seem steep and difficult. With familiarity and practice, however, they will become less daunting. The more you use these steps, the more refined they become, and the more swiftly and fully you will likely move toward accepting The Great Invitation.

The four steps are:

- Envision it.

- Name it.

- Give it.

- Release it.

I encourage you to climb these steps, detailed below.

Envision It.
Name it.
Give it.
Release it.

The envisioning process involves nothing more than self-reflection. You acknowledge your burdens and weariness, whatever they may be. Please do this reflecting without input from others, as their comments could be distracting or unhelpful.

Clearly identify your weariness and burdens. Make note of them all, one by one, either in a mental list or in a written or typed one.

No matter how you create your list, don't dwell on any item or—for now—spend any time editing the list. Just clearly identify what is causing you to be weary and burdened.

Here are a few sample lists to help you start your own envisioning.

From Sara Jane, a teenage girl

- My mom
- My brother and my sister
- Lisa
- Sally
- Pressure to earn good grades
- Pressure to look good
- Anxiety about how much my parents fight over money
- Pressure to please my boss so I don't lose my job
- Pressure to lose weight.

From Lin, a 22-year-old man

- My parents' meddling
- Trying to figure out whom to trust, and when to trust them
- Trying to find my place in life and the world
- All my student debt, and uncertainty about how I am going to pay it off
- Andrew's recent betrayal
- The upcoming election and its effect on my friends and family.

The Greatest Invitation

From Demont, a 41-year-old man

- My parents' declining health
- My hour-long commute
- My neighbor's dog
- Always adjusting family time to meet our kids' schedules
- Our financial obligations
- The fear of me or Jayla losing our jobs—what would we do???
- Seeing how well some of our friends are doing, and feeling inept and inferior
- Wanting but not getting enough time to myself
- Always having to defend myself because of my dark skin
- Daily and increasing frustration in my job.

From Ruth, an 84-year-old woman

- Seeing my mother staring back at me in the mirror
- Worry about my children and grandchildren
- Feeling like I'm often shoved to the side
- There's no one I can truly confide in anymore
- Unmet goals and unrealized dreams
- The future of our country and world
- Where to get the money to pay for both food and medications
- I thought that at this age, things would be resolving; instead, I'm worried about more things now than when I was a teen.

If you have never done this kind of envisioning before, the process itself can lead to a brief euphoria. You may think, *Finally, I'm getting somewhere.* This euphoria is natural and commonplace.

It may lead you to feel that things are going to get better quickly. For some, that may even happen—temporarily.

However, if you don't move beyond the envisioning step, that euphoria will soon dissipate—and you are not likely to realize the gifts that await you from accepting The Great Invitation. So, do feel good about taking the first step, yet remember, it is only the first step.

Don't pressure yourself to complete this envisioning within some arbitrary timeframe. It's important to do it at your own pace, so that it doesn't add to your burdens. It's fine to start the list, set it aside, and come back to it later. As you'll see, it's also fine to alter the list at a later time, after further reflection. How you create the list is up to you—but work on it until you feel you have completed it.

ENVISION what makes you weary or is weighing you down. Make a mental or physical list of these things.

Envision it.
Name It.
Give it.
Release it.

The next step is naming. This involves two phases: first, reflecting on the burdens and sources of weariness that you've listed and, second, applying a name.

Reflecting

Now it's time to edit, change, add to, or delete from your list. Question and dig deeper into the items you have identified.

Are there any items that are related in some way? Can you group these together? Are there items that are variations of one or two major sources of weariness? Do you see a deeper issue or connection that hadn't occurred to you before? Is there something you would now add or delete?

As you reflect, you may be tempted to rush through the list in order to move quickly into assigning names. If so, stop and ask yourself: *Where is the pressure to rush coming from? Are there any burdens or sources of weariness that I've overlooked, or been avoiding?* Remember, take whatever time you need.

Here are some examples of how others have discovered insights through their reflection:

- Sara Jane listed *My mom* and *my brother and my sister.* After some reflection, she grouped them together under *My family.* Then she thought about it some more, and realized that the underlying burden was *Mom's failing health.*

- Lin listed *Trying to figure out whom to trust, and when to trust them* and *Andrew's recent betrayal.* After reflecting, he grouped the two together as *Pain and difficulty in trusting others.*

- Demont's list included *My hour-long commute.* After thinking about that item, he realized that the real burden wasn't the time involved, but being the driver for his carpool on Fridays.

- As Ruth reflected on her list, she realized that she hadn't listed a burden she'd been carrying for decades: her grief over her failed marriage. She had carried that burden so long that it had become second nature to her. She added it to her list.

Here is an example of how this reflection process can evolve:

CAROLYN

When Carolyn made her mental list, she focused on the burden of completing projects at work. As she explored her feelings and memories, she realized that the burden wasn't so much the work itself, or even the deadlines for completing it, but the strain and tension she put on herself for finishing every project on time and in the way she wanted it to be: perfect.

Then she realized that she was overlaying her perfectionism onto all of her projects, including those for her family and all of her volunteer efforts. All of this only increased the weight of her burden, especially when several projects had deadlines that were close together. The issue was not completing her projects at work, as she had once thought, but an internal issue of her own making.

At first she felt that she was finally ready to name her burden: *perfectionism.* But that didn't seem quite right, so she gave herself the time for further consideration. This additional reflection gave rise to a profound question: *Why am I a perfectionist in the first place?*

As she probed her own motivations, she was eventually able to name her deeper, underlying burden: her fear of failure.

Applying a Name

Notice how Carolyn's answer to that question moved her from simply reflecting on her situation to naming her underlying burden. This demonstrates how important this process of naming can be.

There are times when, for whatever reason, we are unable to put our finger on what is bothering, unsettling, or disturbing us. We know something isn't right, but it remains undefined and unresolved. This can leave us feeling powerless, weary, and over-burdened. We then become further burdened by not knowing precisely what our burden is.

But when we finally can give a name to our burden, we begin to assume a position of power over it.

In Genesis 2:19, Adam names the animals. This verse is less about animals getting their names and more about the Bible teaching us about the power of naming. If you can name something, it means you have moved to a position of power in relation to it. It means that now you can do something about it and with it.

In Twelve Step programs such as A.A., one of the first essential steps for an addict is their admission that they have an addiction and are powerless over it. When a person freely says, "I am an addict," they are then in a position of power to move forward with their recovery.

Similarly, when you can name each burden or source of weariness, you become empowered to live into The Great Invitation.

Here are a few examples of how people came to name their own burdens and sources of weariness:

- Carolyn, who felt burdened by her perfectionism, named her real burden: *fear of failure.*

- Sara Jane, the teenager who listed *Lisa* and *Sally* on her envisioning list, crossed out both those names, then wrote *friends.* A few minutes later, she crossed that off and wrote *trust.* After a few more minutes, she landed on the most accurate name for her burdens: *untrustworthy friends.*

- After Demont created his list, he realized that he was at a pivotal point in his life. After further reflection, he realized that he was feeling more and more unfulfilled in his job. He finally arrived at naming his burden: *Not living my heart's desire.*

NIA AND TYRONE

By the time Nia was in her early 60s, she had lived with chronic leukemia for several years. Eventually, as her battle with the illness intensified, she moved in with her daughter Emma Jean, her son-in-law Michael, and her five-year-old grandson, Tyrone. Anticipating her final decline, Nia gave Emma Jean and Michael the right to make health care decisions for her.

In time, Nia's health worsened significantly. She spent a few days in the hospital, but was able to return home. Her doctor told Emma Jean and Michael that Nia probably had only a few more months to live. But the doctor did not share this prediction with Nia.

That night, moved by Nia's increasingly fragile condition, Emma Jean and Michael—not wanting Tyrone to say the wrong thing at the wrong time—made the decision to tell Tyrone but not Nia. Amidst hugs and tears, they told Tyrone, "Ty, Nana is getting sicker and very weak. Please be careful around her. She won't be with us too much longer. Ty, she . . . well, she's going to die. So, your Dad and I want to make sure we do as much as we can to make her feel good. This will be our secret—so don't tell Nana. We know this is a hard time—for all of us. So, if you feel sad, come and talk to us. Okay?" Ty nodded.

Soon afterward, Tyrone started acting out in all kinds of ways—throwing tantrums, hurling objects at the wall, or suddenly bursting into tears.

One afternoon, Emma Jean and Michael left Tyrone with Nia to run a couple of quick errands. Almost as soon as the door closed, Tyrone launched into yet another tantrum.

Nia had had enough. She called to Ty determined to get to the bottom of what was going on. She opened her arms and Ty climbed into her embrace.

"Tyrone, you know I love you, honey. You know that you're safe here. You can tell me anything and I'll listen to what you have to say. So, tell Nana—what's going on?"

Tyrone stared into her eyes. "Oh, Nana, I, I . . ." then he dropped his head and said, in a whisper, "I can't."

Nia quickly realized what was probably stopping Tyrone. She nodded and said, "Oh, I see. Tell me, Tyrone, did Momma and Daddy tell you something?"

Tyrone nodded.

"Okay," Nia said, "Does it have to do with me?"

Tyrone raised his head, and his eyes widened. He looked intently—hopefully—at Nia.

"Well, Tyrone, since it's about me, don't you think you and I could talk about it? Just between us?"

At that, Tyrone gave Nia a bear hug, then burst into tears. "I don't want you to die, Nana! I don't want you to die!"

Nia cradled him until Tyrone's sobs subsided. Then she asked, "Is that what Momma and Daddy told you, that I'm going to die?"

Tyrone nodded.

Nia smiled. "Tyrone, I already know that. So you see, Momma, Daddy, you, and I, we all know. Now, there's nothing we can do to keep me from dying, but it probably won't happen today, or this week, or even this month. And now, since we all know, no one has to keep any secrets about it any longer. We can focus on living with the time we have."

Once the whole family—including Tyrone—could name the secret, they all had the power to deal with it. And, as a family of faith, they soon began to pray together about Nia's condition.

With the encouragement of others, including their pastor, the whole family was able to give Nia's illness to Jesus.

> NAME each weariness and burden, so that you move to a place of power over it.

Envision it.
Name it.
Give It.
Release it.

This third step—the heart of this process—is giving every burden and all your weariness to Jesus. Take all of it off yourself and give all of it to him.

Come to me, all you who are weary and are carrying heavy burdens, and I will give you rest. The Great Invitation is crystal clear: Jesus asks you for all those things that make you weary and burdened. He doesn't want you to hang onto or haul around anything that can diminish, distort, or damage your life. He understands how such weight can hamper your ability to live freely and fully.

In return for giving those things to him, Jesus offers you the fullness of rest, and a renewed and refreshed life.

But you cannot give your weariness and burdens to Jesus if you:

- pretend they don't exist—or deny that they do
- numb yourself through drugs, alcohol, overwork, inappropriate sex, or addictive behavior
- try to hide your weariness and burdens from others, from yourself, or from God.

Paradoxically, giving your weariness and burdens to Jesus requires that you first claim ownership of them. You claim them as yours so you can give them away.

Here is a story of someone who suddenly was able to own his weariness and burdens, then give them to Jesus.

PASTOR STEVE AND REBECCA

Like most young pastors in their early years of ministry, Pastor Steve knew that many people would come to him with their problems. What he wasn't prepared for was the quantity, intensity, and diversity of them. They felt like a never-ending flood.

Neither was he prepared for how so many people would not talk with him until they were in crisis. Then they needed his advice, counsel, and answers—right now!

Still, he thought that he was managing the load of others' burdens fairly well.

That illusion came crashing down at a late-night dinner with his wife Rebecca and their nine-year-old son Jason.

They sat at the table in near silence. Steve stared down at his plate, moving his food around instead of eating it. That morning, he had discovered that his pastoral mentor and his wife, both of whom were instrumental in him becoming a pastor, were divorcing. A few hours later, a trusted lay leader in his congregation told him that she and her husband were splitting up and both moving out of town.

Rebecca spoke, breaking his reverie. "Steve, what's wrong?"

He sighed. "Oh, so many people have come to me this week. Then came the news that Pastor Mike and Diane are getting a divorce. And now it's Janice and Tim—and, if that weren't bad enough, both of them are moving away. All four have meant so much to me."

Steve expected some words of empathy and compassion from his wife. When they didn't come, he looked up from his plate. To his shock, he was looking at her stony face and icy eyes.

"Rebecca, what's wrong?"

The silence continued for a few more seconds. Then she erupted. "What's wrong, you ask? *What's wrong? Look at the clock!* It's another night when you get home after 8 and we eat dinner at 9.

Look at Jason—he's half asleep! He and I are at the table with you, but we might as well be eating in Timbuktu, for all the attention you're giving us. It's always *that* person's troubles, or *those* people's problems. They take up more and more of your time and spirit. Meanwhile, Jason and I just get the leftovers.

"I've had it! What's wrong? *We* are wrong. If Diane and Janice had to put up with what Jason and I are dealing with, then I can understand why they're divorcing! Something has to change!"

Rebecca rose from the table, walked angrily to their bedroom, and slammed the door.

The silence was deafening. Finally, Jason broke the stillness, his voice quavering. "Daddy, why is Mommy so angry?"

In the days that followed The Dinner, as Steve would later call it, he did much soul-searching. He realized he had been carrying everyone else's burdens—as well as his own—all by himself. "Something has to change," Rebecca had said. *Yes*, he came to realize, *something does have to change. I have to change.*

On the heels of that admission, Jesus' words from Matthew came to him: *Come to me all you who are weary and carrying heavy burdens . . .*

Steve went to his Bible, found the passage, and read it over and over. With each re-reading, it sunk in deeper. He thought, *Jesus wants me to give him my weariness and burdens—every burden, mine and others', that I've been carrying around.*

Well, if Jesus wants them, he can have them. If that is his Invitation, I'm ready to accept.

In that moment, something shifted inside Steve. Right then, and from that time forward, Pastor Steve made a point of giving all his weariness and all his burdens to Jesus.

That one shift renewed his family and transformed his life.

*****

How, exactly, do we hand over our weariness and burdens to Jesus? We can't mail him a letter, send him a text, or fill out an online form.

As you've seen already in all the stories in this book, what we can do is pray.

In many of these stories, people's prayers have been spontaneous, unstructured, and suited to the particular moment. But you can also use more deliberate, structured forms of prayer.

In the pages that follow, I offer four types of prayer that you can use. Choose whichever ones most resonate with you. Feel free to experiment with or adapt each one—but keep in mind two things:

- You may need to use the prayer repeatedly, not just once.

- The purpose of each form of prayer is to help you give your weariness and burdens to Jesus.

Prayers of Self-Emptying

These prayers empty you of the weariness and burdens that have filled you up.

Use a Bible verse.

Recite—say or sing—a verse, or a portion of a verse, aloud or silently. Repeat the words over and over. This repetition provides both inspiration and reinforcement.

You may recite the verse many times in succession, over several minutes, or recite it only once each time, but multiple times throughout your day. Some people find it valuable to recite their chosen verse the moment they wake up and immediately before going to sleep.

Here are a few sample verses you can use:

> Cast your burden on the Lord and he will sustain you.
> —*a portion of Psalm 55:22*

> Cast all your anxiety on him, because he cares for you.
> —*I Peter 5:7*

> And going a little farther, he [Jesus] threw himself on the ground and prayed, "My Father, if it is possible, let this cup pass from me; yet, not what I want but what you want."

The Greatest Invitation

—Matthew 26:39

Use a prayer written by others.

Here are some self-emptying prayers that have been used for hundreds of years:

> God of all power, be present in your goodness with me; empower me to give my weariness and burdens to Jesus. Amen.

> Jesus, healer of the wounded and infirm: so fill my heart with trust in your goodness that I may be strengthened to give you my burdens and so make room for your goodness. Amen.
>
> *—Episcopal Book of Common Prayer*

> Christ Jesus, when all is darkness and I feel my weariness and burdens, give me the sense of your presence, love, and strength. Help me to have trust in your protecting love and strengthening power, in giving you all that frightens and worries me. Amen.
>
> *—St. Ignatius of Loyola.*

DEMONT AND JAYLA

After Demont realized that he was not living his heart's desire, he didn't immediately give his weariness and burdens to Jesus.

In fact, several weeks passed. During this time, he often thought about his dilemma, but did nothing about it. As a result, he grew even more weary and burdened. He became fearful and worried about what any potential change in his life might bring.

One day, while doing the supper dishes and ruminating on his burdens, he got so distracted that he cut himself badly with a carving knife. He ended up at an emergency room, where he had to get multiple stitches on his hand.

His wife Jayla, who had been away on an errand, rushed to the hospital to be with him. When Demont told Jayla what had happened, and what was going on in him, she told him, "Dem, you need to pray about this."

Using the burden-lifting prayer from the *Episcopal Book of Common Prayer*, that is exactly what Demont did.

Use your own prayer.

Create—and say, sing, chant, or repeat—your own prayer. It does not have to be long, or flowery, or even grammatically correct. It only needs to express your desire to empty yourself of weariness and burdens and give them to Jesus. It can be as simple as: *Jesus, empty me of my burdens. Amen.*

Here is one of the prayers I wrote for myself:

> *To you, O Jesus, I do pray*
> *to ask your help along this way.*
> *To empty self of burdens great—*
> *things so named from my weary state.*
> *Into your outstretched arms I give*
> *what weighs me down, that I may live. Amen.*

Use a fast.

Although fasting usually involves abstinence from food, and is often connected to health or weight loss, it is also an ancient spiritual practice used to turn a person's focus away from themselves, and toward others and God.

Fasting engages your whole being in the process of self-emptying. Through it you acknowledge and face all the places of fullness in your life.

Through fasting, you empty yourself of your weariness and burdens, so that Jesus can take them. Fasting helps you connect quickly to the gifts offered in The Great Invitation. Now that your arms are empty—especially of your weariness and burdens—they can receive what Jesus wants to give you.

Here are a few guidelines based on this understanding of fasting:

- A fast can involve abstaining from any habitual activity, not just eating and drinking. You can fast from watching television, or using the internet, or lifting weights.

- You cannot fast from something you don't normally eat, drink, or do. If you don't ordinarily eat broccoli or drink coffee, you can't fast from those. But if you regularly eat bread and drink tea, then you can exclude those from your diet.

- How long you fast, and what you fast from, are up to you. You may fast for a day or two, or a week, or longer. Some people choose to fast on a certain day each week. Others fast continuously over a period of several weeks. For example, you might fast from eating sugar, or using social media, or drinking alcohol, from New Year's Day to Easter Sunday.

- Don't do anything that may endanger your physical, mental, or emotional health. For example, in hot weather, or if you do moderate or strenuous exercise, continue to drink enough water. And don't avoid eating for so long that you feel weak or dizzy.

Remember, the point of this fast is to help you give your weariness and burdens to Jesus. Here are two examples of people who used fasts for this purpose:

HECTOR AND ISIDRO

Hector was a devout Christian who made a point of praying for others. Over time, his prayer list grew longer and longer—and he gradually became wearier and wearier. Because he felt obliged to pray for all of these people, eventually he came to resent these prayers. What should have been a source of joy for him became a burden.

But when he thought about not praying for some of the people on his list, he felt guilty. This only added to his burden.

One day his good friend Isidro said to him, "Hector, I know you pray for people. My aunt Isabella is in the hospital with pneumonia. Would you please keep her in your prayers? We'd both appreciate it."

To Hector's own shock, he blurted out, "No! I can't. I'm sorry, Isidro, but I just can't. Not anymore—no more!"

As Hector stared at Isidro's wide eyes and gaping mouth, he realized what he had just said to his good friend. "Oh, Isidro, I'm so sorry! I've just been overwhelmed lately. Please forgive me. Of course, for you, my friend, I will pray."

Afterward, Hector began to examine what was going on for him. He realized that he didn't need to stop praying for others; but he needed to change the *way* he prayed.

He started that change by fasting from lunch one day a week. Instead of eating, he used his lunch hour as time for contemplation. Soon that turned into time for prayer—prayer for others.

After Hector had fasted once a week for a month, the joy of praying for other people returned.

KYOUTO

Kyouto often felt frazzled and exhausted. There were never enough hours in the day to do everything that needed to be done. This frustrated Kyouto greatly, because he had recently retired. He'd expected to feel like he had *more* time, not less. Yet, by the end of the day, after he had run all his errands and completed all his household chores, there was often no time left to connect with friends.

When he complained to his wife Arianna about his situation, she just smiled, shook her head, and said one word: "Golf."

As much as Kyouto hated to admit it, from the beginning of his retirement, playing golf had consumed more and more of his time. He loved the game, but simply did not have the time to play 18 holes every day.

The Greatest Invitation

After saying a few prayers, Kyouto decided to stop golfing for a while and see what happened.

What happened was that, within two weeks, he became ready to ask Jesus to take his burden of being frazzled and exhausted. And when he did, Kyouto found a new and more balanced vision for his life.

This vision didn't exclude golf. After he accepted The Great Invitation, he resumed playing a few times a week. But now spending time with all his friends, and doing necessary tasks around the house, took priority over his golfing.

Kyouto's fast from golfing, and his willingness to accept The Great Invitation, helped him be free from what had become an obsession.

Prayers of Visualization

Our imagination is a powerful creative force. Prayers of visualization can open us in ways that words alone cannot. Here are three forms of such prayers.

Breath meditation

In this simplest form of visualization, simply sit in a quiet space and focus on your breathing. Breathe out, breathe in. Breathe out, breathe in.

As you breathe out, imagine breathing out your weariness and burdens. Feel them leaving your body, being breathed out to Jesus. Breathe them out.

Then, as you breathe in, imagine Jesus breathing into you his rest, joy, and love.

Breathe out your weariness and burdens. Breathe in Jesus' rest, joy, and love. Breathe out, breathe in. Breathe out, breathe in.

As you repeatedly practice this visualization, you will develop the ability to intentionally focus on breathing out and breathing in. You'll be able to do this focused breathing in all kinds of circumstances, not just in a quiet space. At any time, wherever you are, in any moment, you will be able to give your weariness and burdens to Jesus.

Visual meditation

Find a safe, comfortable place where you will not be interrupted. This can be outdoors, in a park or garden, at the beach, or in a forest—or it can be indoors, in an office, at a place of worship, or in a room in your home. Even a bathroom or large closet can work. Your eyes can be either open or closed.

Begin by quieting yourself. Some people do this by repeating a short prayer for several minutes. Others choose to sing a song, or a portion of one. Still others simply sit still, focusing on their breathing. However you choose to begin, the goal is to slow down, focus, and draw inward.

Now imagine yourself holding your burdens. Notice how they feel and what they look like. What size, shape, and colors are they? Do they have a smell? A texture? A temperature?

Next, imagine Jesus coming to you. Note what he looks like, how he is dressed, and the expression on his face. Is he carrying anything? If he speaks—which may or may not happen—listen closely to what he says and how he says it. Whether or not he speaks to you, feel free to speak to him.

Then visualize yourself physically giving what you are holding—your burdens—to Jesus.

Note the details of how this happens. Do you place them in Jesus' arms? Do you lay them at his feet? Does he reach out and take them from you? What, if anything, does he say once he has your burdens?

Next, imagine Jesus leaving with your burdens. As he leaves, what do you feel, sense, or say?

To conclude the visualization, imagine yourself leaving the scene—without your burdens.

Some people do this visualization regularly, at the end of each day, just before they go to sleep. This process enables them to lay down the burdens of that day, every day.

Visualizations from God

The visualizations I've just described are deliberate, planned, and largely self-directed. But sometimes, unexpectedly, people receive visualizations as gifts from God. Here is a true account of one such experience.

POLLY

When I was Polly's spiritual director, she told me several times that she didn't do meditation or visualization. "That's not how I speak with God," she said.

"No problem," I replied. "God comes to us in whatever way we can receive Him."

Then, one day, she arrived for our meeting filled with exuberance. "Wait till you hear what I have to tell you!" she announced. "You won't believe it."

Here is what she told me, in her own words.

This occurred when I was sitting in a chair, attempting, by means of centering prayer, to rid my mind of the resentment that was chewing away at me because of something someone had said at work that I considered to be unfair. Very unfair.

I saw myself standing in a featureless expanse of white, with a large, square yoke of ugly dark wood across my shoulders. It was about 4x6 and not shaped at all. Hanging from each end were wires or ropes going down to square white platforms that were holding piles of bricks. The whole thing was so heavy and uncomfortable that I couldn't move, and for some reason didn't just put it down.

Jesus came walking up. I knew it was him because he looked just like the picture of Jesus with the light brown curly hair I'd seen when I was a kid. He started taking the bricks off, one by one, alternating sides, and tossing them in the air, where they each disappeared in a tiny poof of pink smoke. Then he took off the wires and platforms and set them aside, and then lifted the yoke. He smoothed it with his hands and it became golden, with a dark grain and a soft shine. It was beautiful.

Then he replaced it. It fit perfectly and wasn't heavy at all. Then he picked up the platforms by the wires and walked away. Nothing was said, but when he got a little ways away, he turned slightly toward me and waved with his left hand, as if to say, 'Think nothing of it.'

Of course, without the wires and platforms, I can't pick up the resentment again.

Active Prayers

Active prayers are prayers that you offer while you are engaged in some activity. For example, Celtic spirituality is grounded in prayers that people recite while doing daily chores. The Celts prayed as they searched for firewood, milked cows, and gathered food for their meals.

Simply doing an activity does not make it prayerful. Nor is the particular activity important (though of course it should be legal and moral), so long as you combine the activity with prayer. This can work with artistic expression, physical exercise, or ordinary daily tasks such as cleaning, taking out the garbage, or raking leaves. The key is using the activity as a means of giving your burdens to Jesus.

How exactly is this done?

First, acknowledge this as your intention. You are doing the activity in order to give your burdens and sources of weariness to Jesus.

Second, do the activity mindfully, wholeheartedly, and unhurriedly, without worrying about doing it perfectly or achieving a particular goal.

Third, stay open to receiving Jesus' response to your intention, so that you may give your burdens to him.

Here are a few examples of what this might look like.

LUIS

Luis is a sculptor. On days when his weariness and burdens have worn him down, he heads to his studio and begins working on a chunk of clay. Rarely does he finish an object; that is not his intent. What does happen is that he prays that the skilled hands of the Creator will re-fashion *him*, taking his weariness and burdens from him.

Sometimes Luis barely gets his hands wet and muddy. Sometimes, without an initial idea of what he might be shaping, a form starts to emerge. However it evolves, in these moments he finds himself being shaped anew, as he gives his burdens to Jesus.

BUDDY

Buddy has serious rheumatoid arthritis in his hands. Yet he loves to work with his hands, and his hobby is carpentry.

When Buddy feels burdened, he takes some wood and begins planing it. As its roughness becomes smooth, Buddy gives his own roughness—his weariness and burdens—to Jesus. He describes this as a carpenter-to-carpenter conversation.

MORGAN

Morgan is an avid runner who participates in many long-distance races. Most of the time when she runs, she has a goal.

But when she is burdened, she lets go of any goal and turns over her run to Jesus. On those occasions, she doesn't time herself or set a specific distance. She simply says to herself, *Today I'm running to Jesus*, and takes off.

During the run, she focuses on each step bringing her closer to Jesus, reaching him, and giving him her burdens. She finds these runs deeply refreshing.

MEI

Mei is a book author who spends much of her time reading and writing. Yet there are times when she feels weary and burdened by her writing.

When Mei feels this way, she writes a letter to Jesus in longhand. She tells him what is going on, what she is feeling, and exactly how she is burdened and weary. Then she "sends" the letter to Jesus by burning it, giving her weariness and burdens to him in the process.

This activity not only brings her relief and joy, but it has often provided her with inspiration for her books.

KIARA

Kiara is a homemaker with three school-aged children. Kiara has discovered that, when she is distraught and feeling burdened, the act of washing dishes calms her.

When she feels burdened, Kiara washes the dishes while imagining that her burdens are being washed away. Sometimes, as she stands at the sink, she imagines Jesus washing the feet of his disciples.

When she is done, she looks at the dirty water and imagines that it is filled with her burdens. Then Kiara begins draining the sink. As the water disappears, Kiara lets Jesus take her burdens and drain them all away.

Healing Prayer

Healing prayer includes the direct involvement of others—people who pray with you for your well-being.

The inclusion of others brings to light two key dynamics. The first is trust. You must trust the compassion and good intentions of the people who pray for you. If you are unable to do this, please find different people.

The second key dynamic is confidentiality. As healing prayer is as private as it is intimate, those who pray for you must be willing to do so in confidence. (That is why, in the true story that concludes this step—and in the story of John, Tom, and Mary Ann in Part One—I've changed people's names.)

Healing prayer is practiced in many different ways, depending on the group, church, or denomination. So, before you arrange for any healing prayer, contact the appropriate pastor, priest, or lay minister, who can answer your questions regarding the specific form of this practice. This is especially important if you are seeking healing prayer for the first time.

Although the specific practices may vary widely, all Christian healing is based upon Jesus' own ministry, which involved the healing of body, mind, *and* spirit. Jesus' concern is for the well-being of the whole person. Thus, healing prayer can address all of your needs:

- Any kind of woundedness—physical, mental, emotional, or spiritual
- Anything that fragments you, distorts you, or diminishes you
- Any fear, guilt, despair, or anxiety
- Anything that would make you smaller or less yourself.

This makes healing prayer an ideal way to help you when you feel burdened or weary.

With most forms of healing prayer, you are first asked to say out loud what you feel needs to be healed. Your answer should be honest, forthright, and as clear and specific as possible. (This is another reason why it's so important to identify and name your burdens and weariness.)

If you're uncertain exactly what's behind your weariness and burdens, or you are reluctant to say what's behind them out loud, you may simply say, "I want to give my burdens and weariness to Jesus. Please pray for me to do so, fully and willingly." Jesus knows precisely what is on your heart, even if you or others do not.

There is no set length of time for a healing prayer. It simply needs to feel thorough and sufficient to everyone involved. I have witnessed healing prayers that felt complete after five minutes, and those that lasted over an hour.

Lastly, gentle and loving physical contact is typically a part of healing prayer. You might stand or sit, with other people around you, and they may lay hands on your head or shoulders. This touching of your head or shoulders is meant to be a "canopy of healing" over your whole being. In general, touching other parts of your body is unnecessary, and even inappropriate, no matter what style of healing prayer is being used.

Some people may use a small amount of anointing oil—olive oil that has been prayed over or blessed for healing. This may include making the sign of the cross in oil on your forehead. This touch is often healing in and of itself.

If you do not wish to be touched and/or anointed with oil, simply say so. While the loving touch of others can be a wonderful part of healing prayer, it is not a requirement.

CAMERON

For years, Cameron had attempted to quit smoking. He had tried—and failed—too many times to count.

One day, he showed up at a session led by a spiritual healing team. He felt worn out from his failures and burdened by his lack of resolve. He told the team that he was so exhausted and despairing that he was willing to try anything.

Cameron was totally honest with the healing team who surrounded him. "Everything I've done to quit smoking hasn't worked. A day or two later—well, to be honest, sometimes the same day—I'm back smoking. I have a young daughter, and I want to see her grow up. I need help."

The team nodded their understanding. They placed their hands on Cameron's shoulders and began to pray.

Cameron later described what happened next. "Each person prayed that I be given the courage to give my burden to Jesus. One person prayed for me to be lifted from my addiction. Another prayed for the dismantling of my barriers to quitting. Still another prayed that I be led to decisions that would help me stop smoking. All of them prayed for me to be healed by giving Jesus my burden.

"After that group of people prayed for me," Cameron said, "I walked to my car, took the two packs of cigarettes I had, and threw them in the nearest trash can. I've never looked back and never returned to smoking."

> GIVE your weariness and burdens to
> Jesus without hesitation or regret.

Envision It.
Name It.
Give It.
Release It.

This last step is often the hardest.

For many of us, it is easy to *say* that we will give our weariness and burdens to Jesus, yet very hard to actually release them. We cling to them. We give them up in the evening, only to take them all back in the morning.

Why is releasing our weariness and burdens so hard?

If we have carried a burden for a long time, we may eventually develop a pattern of thinking and living that makes releasing it all the more difficult. We may find ourselves repeatedly sliding back into the well-formed habit of hauling around that burden.

We may want to stay in control. We may see the releasing of our weariness and burdens to Jesus as a sign of weakness. We may feel that releasing our grip somehow makes us a failure. We may think that choosing to give them to *anyone*, even Jesus, reduces our own freedom. In short, we may imagine that we are giving up our power, our integrity, or our freedom.

Nothing could be further from the truth. In fact, the opposite is true: fully releasing our weariness and burdens to Jesus, we *gain* power, integrity, and freedom. We become empowered to exercise our gifts and talents, and to live more fully into our humanity. No longer struggling under the oppressive weight of our burdens, we are able to become the person we desire to be. Released from the constraints of our weariness, we experience a new freedom.

We may also struggle to accept that Jesus truly *wants* our burdens. His offer sounds too good to be true—and, like many people, we've learned that anything that *sounds* too good to be true usually is.

All the accounts presented in this book demonstrate otherwise.

So do two events in Jesus' life that are recorded in Scripture. In these, Jesus clearly moves beyond what might be expected, and fully takes on another's weariness and burdens.

The Healing of the Paralytic: Mark 2:1–12

In this account, four men bring a paralytic to Jesus to be healed, so that he may walk.

In those days, the man's plight would have been understood to be the result of his sin—or, perhaps, even the sin of his parents. His burden is, of course, his paralyzed state, and he is weighed down even more by his sense of the sin in his life.

If Jesus were to choose only to heal this man physically, there still would be the lingering perception of the sin in his life. And if Jesus were to only heal him spiritually, onlookers would doubt that anything at all had occurred. So, Jesus not only heals the man's physical body, but takes from him both the dynamics and the perception of sin. Here is what happened.

The first thing Jesus says to the paralyzed man is, "Your sins are forgiven." In response, Jesus' opponents question his authority to forgive sins. To this, Jesus asks, "Which is easier—to say to the paralytic, 'Your sins are forgiven,' or to say, 'Stand up and take your mat and walk'?"

The answer is that it is easier to *say*, "Your sins are forgiven," because who can prove they aren't? The harder thing to say is, "Stand up and take your mat and walk," because that can be proven. Jesus then says to the paralytic, "I say to you, stand up, take your mat, and go to your home." The once-paralyzed man, now both spiritually and physically healed, stands up and walks out through the crowd.

Jesus' desire was for the man to be fully and completely healed—not only in his own eyes, but in everyone else's. He healed the man spiritually through forgiving his sins *and* accomplished the much more difficult task of healing him physically.

In the same way, Jesus wants *you* to be fully released from your weariness and burdens by giving and releasing them to him.

.

The Healing of a Centurion's Servant: Matthew 8:5–13

The central figure in this Biblical story is a centurion, a despised leader of Roman troops—and a non-Jew. Centurions were known to be ruthless and brutal in conduct. If anyone might warrant Jesus' dismissal, it would be a centurion.

This centurion comes to Jesus to plead for the healing of one of his servants. In response, Jesus not only does not dismiss the centurion, but heals the servant.

This passage demonstrates that Jesus is willing to take on *anyone's* weariness and burdens, no matter who asks, or who receives the benefit, or what is involved.

In short, releasing your burdens and weariness to Jesus is *not* too good to be true. It is very good, *and* it is very true.

DEMONT AND JAYLA

For several weeks, Demont gave his burdens to Jesus, but then kept taking them back again.

Whenever Jayla asked him how he was doing, he would say, "I'm working on it." After a few weeks she stopped asking.

But every day she also prayed that her husband would finally and fully release his burden to Jesus.

One day at work, Demont found himself staring at a report, and realized that he had been reading and re-reading the same page for several minutes. Then, suddenly, it hit him: *I know exactly why I'm so weary. I know that I need to give my burdens completely to Jesus, once and for all. I know that Jayla wants me to. I know that Jesus wants me to. And I want desperately to be unburdened. But I'm frightened. I don't know what will happen. But I have to trust that wherever this goes, Jesus will continue to provide mercy for me and my family.* He sighed deeply. *Okay, Jesus. I know that the key to my future, and my family's future, is to let go of this burden. Help me now.*

He breathed in, then breathed out in a whisper, "Jesus, here is my burden. Give me strength to walk a new path."

A few minutes later, Demont's phone rang. The caller was Nate, an old friend who owned a successful business. "Demont," Nate said, "you've been on my mind recently. There's an opportunity here that's opened up, and it seems to me that you're exactly the right person for it. It's a little different from what you've been doing, but I think you have the right qualities and skills. Would you be willing to come in and interview for it?"

And so Demont's new path—and new life—began. The burden and weariness that came from not living his heart's desire evaporated, like dew in the morning sun.

Alex

For years, Alex had wrestled with a deeply painful memory from when he was seven. On a warm spring day, after Alex's father picked him up from school, he told Alex that he needed to drop off something at his boss's house. As his dad parked the car, he said, "Stay in the car, Alex. This shouldn't take long. I'll be right back. Okay?" Alex nodded and rolled down his window to smell the nearby lilacs.

Alex's dad walked to the front door, rang the bell, and was ushered inside. A minute or two later, Alex began to hear his dad's boss yelling at his dad, calling him all sorts of names. Then he heard his father explaining something to his boss in a calm, even voice, but that only made his boss angrier. He wouldn't stop yelling.

Then a woman started yelling, too. "You're a moron, Tony!" Alex heard her say. "I don't know why my husband doesn't fire you!"

After another minute or so, the door to the house opened. Alex expected his father to walk outside, but instead a woman his father's age stepped out. When she saw Alex in the car, she headed quickly down the drive and stopped at Alex's open window, her face twisted in anger. She pointed an accusing finger at Alex and half-shouted, "Your father is a total loser! And you know what? That makes you a loser, too." Then she stormed away into the open garage.

A few minutes later, Alex's dad emerged from the house, his expression grim but calm. He got in the car and they drove home together in silence.

Alex was now 37. He had a job as a software engineer that he liked and was good at, and he had just gotten engaged. He was mostly happy with his life. Yet, every time Alex remembered the rant of "the evil boss's wife," as he referred to her, he would inwardly cringe. The memory of her words still ripped a hole in his soul.

For over 30 years, Alex had never talked to anyone about this vivid and painful memory. He didn't bring it up to his parents (even after his father had taken a new and better job a few weeks later); or to his older brother Bill; or even to his fiancée. He kept the memory bottled up inside, along with his grief and anger.

To Alex's surprise, after his 37th birthday, that memory started coming to him more and more often, in every vivid detail.

Finally, he told his friend Kevin, a caring and discreet confidant. As Alex related his story, tears streamed down his cheeks. "I've been carrying this memory around like a ball and chain for decades," he said.

Kevin listened intently. Then he expressed his sorrow, support, and compassion. Then he asked, "Do you want to lay down this anger and grief?"

"Oh, God, yes," Alex said. "I don't want to carry it anymore."

"Good," Kevin said. "Jesus doesn't want you to carry it anymore, either."

Alex stared at Kevin in stunned silence. It had never occurred to Alex that Jesus would not want him to carry the burden. "Really?"

Kevin nodded. "Really! Jesus loves you, Alex. He wants what is best for you and carrying this burden around is certainly not what is best for you—your tears tell me that the experience is still holding you hostage. Now, you may never forget the incident, but you shouldn't be held hostage to it. You don't want that, and Jesus doesn't want that, either."

"So, what do I do?" Alex asked.

After some further conversation, Kevin gave Alex these instructions: "Now, close your eyes. You described your anger and grief as a ball and chain, so imagine them in that way. See them. Feel them attached to you, holding you down. Now tell Jesus what you want to do with that ball and chain. Speak to him just like you're doing with me."

Alex sat in silence for a few moments. Then he drew a long breath and started talking. "Uh, Jesus, I'm in a lot of pain here. I have been for a long time. It feels like a ball and chain. It's become so heavy. I can't drag it around anymore. Please take it from me. I don't want it back, ever. Take it, forever."

Kevin replied as softly as he could, "Let Jesus take it. Let him take it all. Watch him take it from you. Watch him leave with it. And then tell yourself, 'Not carrying this anymore is good for me.' Repeat that several times to yourself."

Alex did.

Then Kevin said, "Over the next week, repeat that phrase several times a day: 'Not carrying this anymore is good for me.'"

On that day, Alex released his pain and grief to Jesus.

Today, Alex can talk about that childhood experience without anger or grief. In fact, Alex, has been able to use that experience as a way to better empathize with others.

****

How will you know that you have fully released your own weariness and burdens?

The answer has to do with power. Do the sources of your weariness and burdens still wield any power over you? Do they still shape your decisions and actions in some way?

If your answer is no, then you have given and released your burdens to Jesus. If the answer to either question is yes, then you are still holding on to them in some way.

Some people find that they don't need to ask, *How will I know?* They unequivocally *feel*, in their bodies and hearts, that Jesus has taken their burdens and weariness from them.

> RELEASE any remaining hold on what you have given to Jesus, so that you can go forward, refreshed and renewed.

PART THREE

Living into The Great Invitation

ONCE YOU HAVE ACCEPTED The Great Invitation, you can expect to receive three gifts: rest, the yoke of joy, and the burden of love.

Each of these gifts fills the space where weariness and burdens once held sway. Each brings transformation and hope, which may overflow into the lives of those around you.

Jesus gives these gifts in abundance, with no limitation or expiration date. Each gift also opens us to receive:

- greater empowerment in living more fully
- a refreshing of our life that can continuously grow in us—and in our relationships
- a never-ending resource of goodness.

As you receive these gifts, you will discover that rest creates the capacity for hope; joy creates a pathway to hope; and love creates a place in which hope grows.

Rest

As we've seen, this rest positively impacts our whole being, bringing restoration to our bodies, tranquility of mind, and serenity of spirit. It does this in two ways.

First, it removes the compounding negative effects of our weariness and burdens. These negative effects typically include interference with sleep, reduced alertness and brain function, increased cardiac risk, and the impairment of our immune system. Weariness and burdens can also increase anxiety, worry, frustration, and impatience (with others *and* with ourselves). They diminish our creativity, as well as our energy and vigor for life.

Second, this rest gives us compounding relief, refreshment, and renewal—all of which increase our capacity for hope. We become strengthened to meet the day, supported to handle our challenges, and empowered to be more discerning and creative. We become energized and invigorated. We receive a foundation for peace, imagination, courage, perseverance, and, of course, hope.

HENRY

Henry was at his wit's end. He could feel life closing in on him. Suzi, his five-year-old daughter, lay in a pediatric intensive care unit, battling for her life. At first he had thought that Suzi—who complained of not feeling well—might have eaten something that disagreed with her. But when she didn't get better for two days, he took her to their doctor, who told him that Suzi had the flu. Henry thought that she had gotten a flu shot, but when the doctor checked her medical record, they discovered that she had not.

Then complications developed. Suzi's fever of 102 wouldn't go down. After several days, pneumonia set in, requiring her to be given oxygen. Then she developed a dangerous case of sepsis.

Now Suzi lay in a hospital bed, hooked up to oxygen, multiple monitors, and IVs containing all kinds of fluids. Just the sight of it horrified Henry.

Throughout all this, questions hounded him: How had he somehow overlooked getting her a flu shot? How could he have been so careless? What else had he done wrong as a father? Was God punishing his daughter for his mistakes? Surely, Suzi hadn't done something to deserve this illness, had she? What was God's role in all this? Indeed, where was God in his and Suzi's lives?

What more could be done? Why wasn't she responding? How was he going to pay for all this? Why did it seem as if the doctors were always playing catch-up instead of staying ahead of her illness?

Trying to sleep by her bedside had proven to be a lost cause. Henry tossed and turned all night, and couldn't concentrate throughout the following day.

As the days passed, Suzi's condition worsened. Henry felt more and more helpless. His hope ebbed away.

One night, as the familiar hounding questions began their nightly pursuit, Henry realized he was gradually losing his mind. Soon he wasn't going to be able to function at all. And if he couldn't function, what good would he be to his daughter? He desperately missed his wife, who had died of a sudden illness herself, three years earlier. *I've got to do something*, he thought. *But what?*

As that question hung in the air, he heard an internal voice say, "Come to me."

As a person of faith, that phrase was all he needed to recall the passage from Matthew: *Come to me, you who are weary and carrying heavy burdens, and I will give you rest.*

Henry lay completely still for a few moments as the meaning of The Great Invitation flooded into him. He thought, *I can't carry this alone. I'm a mess. And Suzi needs me. Jesus, I can't go on this way. I need you. I need, I have to give you my burden. So, I do! I give you Suzi's illness. I give you everything connected to her. I give you all the questions I can't answer. Take them from me! Please, Jesus, please. I beg you. Take them from me, now!* Henry repeated those final sentences several times. At long last, he drifted off to sleep.

In the morning, for the first time in days, Henry felt refreshed and renewed. He no longer felt helpless. In fact, somehow, amazingly, he felt empowered.

From then on, whenever the questions knocked at his consciousness, he remembered Jesus' words, repeated them to himself, and gave his burden anew to Jesus.

Soon he became a source of strength and hope for Suzi, and for all the friends, family members, and teachers who loved her.

Learning to give his burdens to Jesus changed the course of Henry's life.

In the end, Suzi recovered completely. Today, as an adult, her childhood battle with the flu is a distant memory in her otherwise healthy life.

Jill

Jill trudged wearily across campus, her eyes fixated on her phone. Because she was looking down, she walked straight into another person, who had tried to step out of her way.

"Oh, I'm sorry," said Jill. Then she got a good look at the person she had plowed into. "Oh, Chaplain Elena! I'm so sorry!"

"I'm okay, Jill, but you might want to watch where you're walking. Someone could really get hurt. Possibly even you. Talk on the phone while you walk, but wait until you're sitting down or standing still to look at your screen."

"Good advice," Jill said. "I'll do that."

"How are things going?" Elena asked. "I haven't seen you around much this semester."

"Oh, I'm, ah, fine," Jill said. Then she paused. "No. Actually, I'm not fine. And I guess I shouldn't be lying to a chaplain."

"Well, you wouldn't be the first—or the last, for that matter. So, what's been troubling you?"

"Well, I have this huge mid-term coming up in one of my biology classes—and I'm a biology major. I haven't been doing well in the class from the start. So, I'm kinda freaking out about it." Jill found herself nervously shifting her feet. "I haven't been sleeping all that well, or eating right. I've started drinking coffee all day, just to get me through, and I'm not even that big a fan of coffee. On top of all that, I caught a terrible cold that doesn't seem to be going away. I'm just so worried about this mid-term. And then, today, my roommate told me that I'm driving her crazy with my anxiety." Jill shook her head. "I just can't . . ."

Elena reached out and took Jill's hand. "We all get that way sometimes. Tell me, have you prayed about this?"

"Yes, I have! But I have to tell you, Chaplain Elena, it doesn't seem to work. I've prayed when I've had other tests, but it hasn't stopped me from worrying, and I don't feel like it helps me while I'm taking the test, either. Maybe I'm just not cut out for prayer."

Elena smiled. "Perhaps you aren't asking what you really need to ask. A lot of students tell me they pray about a test, but it turns out that they want God to magically pour the information into their heads. God isn't going to do your work for you. If that's what you've asked for in your prayers, you might want to do something different."

Jill let the chaplain's words sink in. "Okay," she said finally. "Like what?"

"First, Jill, take what you have—which is your worry and nervousness and sleeplessness—and give them to Jesus. Ask him to take them from you. Then ask him to give you peace. Peace before the test, so you can study well, and not drive your roommate crazy, and peace during the test, so you can truly do your best. Try that for your prayers."

Jill said skeptically, "Okay . . . I'll try."

Chaplain Elena squeezed Jill's hand. "Good. Let me know how it goes."

Later that day, Jill thought back on the conversation. She was still doubtful, but she thought, *Hey, nothing else has worked. Might as well give it a shot.*

A few weeks later, Jill showed up at Elena's office and poked her head inside. As she'd hoped, the chaplain was alone, working at her desk. "Chaplain Elena, I've got some news to tell you!"

"Jill! Come in. Tell me, what's the news?"

"Well, do you remember what you told me before my huge mid-term?"

"I sure do. So, what happened?"

"Well, I have to say, at first I really wasn't sold on your suggestion, but I did do it. I asked Jesus to take all of my worry and anxiety from me. And that first night, that very first night, I got a whole night's sleep! And every night after that, too. I felt better during the day, so I didn't need to drink coffee like before. I even started eating better. I was able to concentrate right up until the mid-term, and I was rested for it, too. And guess what?"

"You passed?"

"I passed with a B+, the best grade I've gotten in that class all term! I just wanted to stop in and say thank you. You made a big difference in my life."

Elena smiled. "Well, you're welcome, Jill, but I really think releasing your burdens to Jesus is what made the difference."

Joy: The Easy Yoke

Joy is not a synonym for happiness. Happiness is temporary, fleeting. When our circumstances change, happiness can quickly turn into sadness, anger, misery, or despair—anything but happiness.

Joy goes far deeper. It is a sign of God's presence, and it is independent of external circumstances. We can be immersed in joy even when we're in the midst of trials, conflicts, hostility, or pain.

In his letter to the Philippians (4:4), Paul urges his readers to: *Rejoice in the Lord always; again I will say, Rejoice.* That letter was written from prison. He wanted the Philippians to experience that same joy in Jesus he was experiencing, even—or maybe because of—where he found himself.

Paul's imprisonment would not have been a happy experience. But even in the midst of his unhappy circumstances, he could experience and exude joy—and he was able to desire that joy for his readers.

This yoke, the joy of God's presence, creates a pathway to hope. With it you know you are not alone. Through it you are given God's power for life. From it come God's graces, flowing continually and abundantly. You are no longer helpless or powerless.

MARIA

For years, Maria was troubled by a dark foreboding whenever an extended family event drew near. In the days leading up to each event, she would sleep fitfully. Sometimes she felt as if a cement block had been tied around her neck. Yet she was unable to figure out the reason behind these dreadful feelings.

Then, one fall, with Thanksgiving and a huge family gathering on the horizon, Maria couldn't live with the painful emotions any more. She made an appointment to see a local pastor and told him about the cement block and her dread. The two of them agreed that they would meet over the next several weeks to explore what might be behind her feelings.

For the first couple of times they met, the two talked about Maria's childhood—but nothing of significance seemed to happen. Then, in their third session, the pastor said, "Maria, you've mentioned the same family picnic several times now—the one from when you were ten or eleven. So why don't you tell me more about that picnic?"

Maria thought for a moment, then opened her mouth—but nothing came out. The pastor's question had unlocked a deep, dark, hidden event buried in her memory.

Suddenly the unlocked images flooded her mind, filling her body with horror and grief. Tears welled up in her eyes and flowed down her face.

After regaining her composure, she began to speak of the unspeakable, in a halting yet determined voice. "When I was a young girl," Maria recalled, "I was raped by my uncle. It first happened at that picnic. But then it happened several more times." She paused and wiped her face. "He's dead now. I think the reason I buried it, the reason . . ." She paused again, then said in a near-whisper, "The reason is, I told my parents, but neither one would believe me. I felt I had nowhere to turn. I had no one I could confide in. So, until I could resist him, I put it out of my mind. Until now."

This recollection was Maria's first step in healing. But the reclaimed memories did not release her burden; they only changed it—from a heavy dread to deep grief and anger.

At her next appointment, Maria told the pastor, "Just like you suggested, I've contacted a counselor, to help me work through my grief and anger. But I also need to tell you something else. In remembering what happened, I realized that I now have a decision to make. I can let that event completely ruin my life. I can hate my family. But, you know what? That won't solve anything. It won't change what happened. And I won't be any better.

"So, I told Jesus that he would have to carry my anger and grief from now on. And he told me that yes, he would.

"Then I told him that the only way I could heal would be by helping other women who'd had the same kind of thing happen to them."

Maria smiled firmly and confidently. "This may sound strange, but ever since I told Jesus that, I've been filled with joy. And it will be my joy to see other women's lives healed, too."

ISAAC

Isaac grew up in a poor, violent neighborhood in a large southern city. Many of the people he knew either did drugs or sold them on the street. As an African American male, he routinely received slurs and insults, and he was often stopped, questioned, and sometimes harassed by the police.

But Isaac was determined to make a decent life for himself. He did well in school and attended church regularly. After graduation, he went straight to college and joined a fraternity, where he made many close friends. He also continued attending church on a regular basis and found time to do volunteer tutoring and other charity work. He felt that his life was on the right track and that his future would be bright.

Then Isaac's closest fraternity brother, Marion, and two of his other friends were murdered by strangers. The killings were as brutal as they were senseless.

At first, the murders crushed Isaac's spirit. His grief was overwhelming. As the days passed, he became steadily more angry with God. *How could you let this happen?* he prayed. *I thought you loved us. I thought you loved me.*

But Isaac didn't just ask these questions of God. He also opened himself to receive God's answers.

For many weeks, he felt especially low, and his grief and anger were extremely keen. As weeks followed weeks, he wondered whether God was paying any attention to him at all.

One night, as he was watching a rainstorm, he unexpectedly received his answer. God's words broke through his internal tempest: *Isaac, if you had been killed with Marion, what would have been your destiny? Your volunteer work is a blessing. Because you are still alive, you can further spread that blessing.*

God continued: *You do not get to decide who lives and who dies. But you can choose how to live. How you live determines what matters about your dying. In serving Me, as Jesus leads you, you choose life.*

That's when Isaac received and accepted The Great Invitation. He turned over all of his burdens to Jesus—his grief, his anger, his shock, his dismay, his questions, his painful *and* pleasant experiences, and all the difficulties of being a living, breathing human being.

That was also when Isaac discovered God's presence everywhere—in all of his life, in all of the universe, in every unfolding moment.

In releasing all of his burdens to Jesus, Isaac gained the entire universe. As Isaac says, "I have the joy of knowing that God is in the moment with you—and with me. That makes all the difference."

Love: The Light Burden

The third gift we receive in accepting The Great Invitation is love. The famous "Love Passage" from First Corinthians describes the dynamics of love this way (13:7):

> *It*
> *bears all things,*
> *believes all things,*
> *hopes all things,*
> *endures all things.*

Love makes life possible and bearable—even in situations that appear to be impossible or unbearable. Love can be found in emergency rooms, intensive care wards, and neo-natal units. Love can be present in times of trauma, destruction, war, and upheaval—even in the moment of death.

Love provides energy and strength, courage and fortitude, discernment, and creativity. Love is the soil in which hope grows.

Yet love is not without risks and challenges. The burden of love stretches us beyond ourselves to become more than we are now. It moves us to acknowledge and respond to the needs of others—sometimes even those of our enemies. It emboldens us to engage in acts of mercy and compassion. It encourages us to place the needs of another before—or beside—our own.

We see this burden of love over and over in our everyday experience:

- In parents who make sacrifices so their children receive what they need.

- In adult children who assist their aging parents as they sicken and die.

- In victims who choose to forgive their offenders.

- In volunteers who work for the well-being of others, with no expectation of reward.

- In anyone who performs an act of kindness or selflessness, and—even when they are criticized for their actions—continues with those acts of kindness.

- In people who stop what they are doing in the wake of a disaster, to help in whatever ways they can.

The truth of the Love Passage reveals itself when there are challenges to face, sacrifices to be made, or hurdles to leap over. Love gives us strength to bear all of these, the resolve to move forward, the vision to see hope, and the perseverance to endure.

As I have witnessed, the giving of love enables us to receive even more love. Shouldering the joyful burden of love empowers us to accept still more of that love.

MAKAYLA

Makayla dropped onto her knees on the kitchen floor and began to cry great, sobbing tears. Strewn around her were broken teacups and saucers. Behind her, she heard the door slam as her workaholic, alcoholic husband hurried away, cursing her and their children.

Slowly, she pulled herself to her feet. She walked slowly to the dining room and sat down heavily at the table, next to a pile of bills.

She could no longer hold the family together. Her husband's pursuit of money and the bottle left no room for her or their children. She knew that her marriage was over and she was now a *de facto* single mother of three. Her world had come crashing down, along with the teacups and saucers.

She knew that if she was going to survive amidst this wreckage, *she* had to change. She didn't know how or in what way; she simply knew that she would have to do something different. Her faith had always been strong, but it was now being tested like never before.

That night, after she put the children to bed, she pulled out her Bible. She read a few passages, then stopped and prayed. She was determined to follow as God guided her, in order to effect the change she knew had to happen.

Through prayer, conversations with her closest friends, and a few visits to her priest, Makayla decided to create a nightly routine. Each night, before sleep, she would give everything to Jesus—the good, the bad, the beautiful, and the ugly. She gave him what delighted her and what weighed on her. She gave him her hope and her despair, her conviction and her uncertainty, her belief and her doubt.

Soon Makayla willingly took on the full burden of love. Over time, this changed her life. She learned not only how to love herself and her children, but her neighbors, people she met for the first time, and strangers.

Over time, she became a person others sought out because they could see love emanating from her and through her.

Makayla's challenges, hurdles, and trials continued. She still had to care for her family. She still had to recover from the marriage that had almost destroyed her and her children. In fact, for a time, the misery created by her husband's addictions grew worse.

Nevertheless, Makayla changed. Day by day, the burden of love gave rise to strength, resolve, vision, and perseverance. Day by day, Makayla learned to live through what once had torn her down—and into a new life of hope and possibility.

DIANE

Diane sat alone in the doctor's exam room, waiting for the nurse to return. Her world had just collapsed. A few minutes earlier, her doctor had told her that she had breast cancer.

Her palms were sweaty. Her thoughts raced in every direction. In the silence of the room, she heard the thumping of her heart.

"We've caught this early," the doctor had said. "There's a lot that we can do to treat it. You should have every expectation of being a cancer survivor."

Yet, Diane thought, *not everyone survives.* Her mind filled with a chorus of *what ifs. What if they can't get all of it? What if it gets worse? What if I go through all of this and the cancer still returns? What if it shows up in someplace new? What if, what if, what if . . .*

That chorus was soon joined by a second chorus of mental accusers, which challenged the foundations of her faith: *God is not with you. God doesn't care. God doesn't really love you. You don't matter to God.*

During the weeks that followed, these choruses would often erupt in the middle of the night, while Diane tried unsuccessfully to sleep. They would interrupt as she drank her mid-morning coffee, or when she put up her feet for a few minutes in the late afternoon.

Soon Diane felt overwhelmed by these voices and burdened in ways she had never experienced.

Finally, she had had enough. *I can let this news and let my mental accusers rule the day, or I can find where God and God's love are in this. Jesus, help me. Take my cancer. Take the what ifs. Take the accusers. I need you. I do believe you love me. Let me live that love.*

These last words quickly became the staple of her life: *Jesus, I do believe you love me. Let me live that love.*

As Diane prayed, day after day, she became her prayer. She found herself becoming the love for which she prayed.

Even during a setback that landed her in the hospital for several weeks, Diane felt immersed in love. She responded to that love by making sure that she prayed for every person who entered her room—every tech, every nurse, every housekeeper, every orderly, every volunteer, every doctor, and every visitor.

Love carried Diane through her healing and recovery. She did become a cancer survivor—and, today, she continues to live into the love that Jesus gifted to her.

Spenser

When Spenser was 13, he and several of his friends attended a summer basketball camp. During some free time, he and his best friend, Brian, were outside, wrestling. Suddenly Brian said, "Hey, Spenser, stop!"

Spenser sat down on the grass. "Yeah?"

"I felt something weird in your belly, above your belly button. Something hard. What the heck is that?"

Spenser looked down. "I don't know, man. I'm supposed to go to the doctor next week to find out."

What Brian had felt turned out to be a tumor from a rare form of cancer called PNET. A week later, Spenser underwent surgery—the first of many.

When Spenser and Brian met after the first surgery, Spenser said, "Okay, the news isn't pretty. The doctors say I might not make it to age 16."

"Crap," Brian said. "What can I do?"

"Plenty," Spenser said.

Soon after his diagnosis, Spenser gave his disease, his battle, all his fears and worries and burdens, and his life to Jesus. He became utterly unburdened.

So, when Brian and others asked him, "What can I do?", he knew what to say. He asked them to bring food for him and his family, and they did. He asked them to hold vigils for him before each surgery, and they did. He asked them to stand with him. So, when Spenser lost his hair, all of his buddies shaved their heads in solidarity.

Spenser also pushed himself, and everyone else he knew, to engage in what was true and meaningful about living.

He survived long enough to graduate from high school. In his address to his graduating class, he reminded everyone, "Once we stop looking *up* the road for satisfaction, and start looking *around* for it, that is when it will come."

Love flowed through Spenser to others, and he encouraged those others to extend that love still further. Spenser's love proved infectious.

Spenser dreamed of being a writer. Through a book published after his death, that love shone through clearly. Here is one of his poems:

> *The more time I spend with God,*
> *the more love I have to give to others.*
> *The more love I give to others,*
> *the more I receive.*
> *The more love I receive, the more time*
> *I want to spend together with*
> *people to love them.*
> *The more I love people, the more*
> *each one of them, even "the*
> *least of my brothers," begins to look*
> *like Jesus.*
> *The more people begin to look*
> *like Jesus, the more I start*
> *looking like the guy.*

A Word of Encouragement

IT IS NOW UP to you.

Accept The Great Invitation; work through the four steps; and receive the gifts that Jesus promised.

But don't just take my word for it.

Here are the words of someone who, like you, heard The Great Invitation and understood that it was for her and everyone, with no exceptions.

ERIKO (IN HER OWN WORDS)

Several years ago, I was beset and quite frankly overwhelmed with burdens. It was driving me crazy and it seemed everything was getting worse.

One day at church, when I was kneeling at the altar rail to receive Communion, I asked Jesus to take my burdens—all of them. I told him, "I can't go on like this. Please take them."

Suddenly I was awash in peace. I could feel them being lifted from me. The Burden-Bearer had taken them from me.

I never looked back.

A Word of Gratitude

THIS BOOK IS THE result of years of reflection and meditation on Jesus' Great Invitation. Everything in it is a gift from God.

My discernment to write grew as the Holy Spirit opened my understanding of Jesus' words and empowered me to live them myself. Then, when Polly told me of her vision, I knew I had to write this book.

Once I became serious about writing it, amazing things began to happen. I reconnected with people whom I hadn't been in contact with for years. I began having dreams related directly to the book. Insights that formed the basis of Part One arose in my prayers. All of Part Two unfolded from being awakened in the middle of the night and having a specific framework revealed to me. Conversations—some that I initiated, and others initiated by a variety of other people—gave me further insights and provided me with ever more stories of people's acceptance of The Great Invitation.

Perhaps most notably, God gave me the words to the prayer below, which I prayed throughout the writing of this book.

Now I offer this prayer to you as well, in honor of God's abundant grace and light:

> Lord Jesus, Shepherd of my soul,
> You are Author of Life and Word of God:
>> Breathe your Spirit
>> into my heart, mind, and will
>> that I may be directed and sustained
>> to convey Your Word through this work
>> to the fulfilling of Your call, grace, and Truth,
>> to the glory of the Father. Amen.

An Invitation to Creativity

THE SUGGESTIONS, STEPS, AND examples offered in this book are intended to provide you with a solid foundation for accepting and living into The Great Invitation.

Yet *you* are the one who must choose what works best for you. Your participation and discernment are required.

In accepting The Great Invitation, please also accept this invitation to creativity.

Here are three examples of this invitation.

Remembering Through Song

It's not always easy to remember prayers or passages from the Bible. But I met a woman named Dorothy who came up with this beautiful solution. She told me, "When I was growing up and going to Sunday school, I was supposed to memorize verses from the Bible. But I just couldn't do it. I don't know why, but they just wouldn't stick. But give me a song to sing, and I could memorize it in a flash and retain it easily. So that's how I learned my Bible verses: I put them to music."

Breath Prayer

A breath prayer is a very brief prayer that can be recited in a single breath. It is meant to be prayed *repeatedly*, throughout the day.

Breath prayers are at once powerful and easily remembered. Alyssa's prayer at the end of Part One, which her family called "Mom's Prayer," is an example of such a prayer.

You can use a line of scripture, or a line from a hymn or song or poem—or you can write a breath prayer (or multiple prayers) of your own.

There are three components to most breath prayers: *a name, an expression of reverence,* and *a plea.*

First, *name to whom you are praying.* Second, *offer your reverence or respect.* Third, *express your specific need.* Ideally, all three components will resonate deeply in your spirit.

The most well-known breath prayer is called The Jesus Prayer:

> *Lord Jesus Christ, Son of God, have mercy on me, a sinner.*

Some examples of people's unique breath prayers include:

> *Jesus, Good Shepherd, lead me into peace.*
> *O God, Source of Being, lift me into hope.*
> *God, help me do Your will.*

You may recite a breath prayer aloud or silently; you may share it with others or keep it strictly private.

Personalizing Scripture

I recommend reciting Jesus' Great Invitation aloud, at least once, each and every day.

I recognize that this can be a challenge in and of itself. And, once we skip a day, that can turn into a week, and then a month. Soon, Jesus' words from Matthew can begin to disintegrate in our memory.

Many people find it helps to personalize the Scripture passage. This can not only help you memorize and recite it, but it enables you to make it your own. Here are some options:

- Add your name to it, so that Jesus addresses you directly.
- Set it to meter or a beat.

- Reword it, perhaps so that it rhymes (but be careful not to change the meaning).

- Emphasize specific parts or aspects of the passage.

- Like Dorothy, set the passage to music and sing it.

Here is my own re-wording of The Great Invitation. This helps me remember that The Great Invitation is for me. It also helps me to remember to recite it and accept it daily:

> *Jesus says to me,*
> *David,*
> *come,*
> *bring your weariness and burdens.*
> *Give them to me.*
> *I will give you rest.*
> *You will be refreshed.*
> *Receive from me my yoke of joy,*
> *my burden of Love,*
> *for they are easy and light.*

This is the end of the book.
It can be the beginning of hope.